Shifting Prophecy

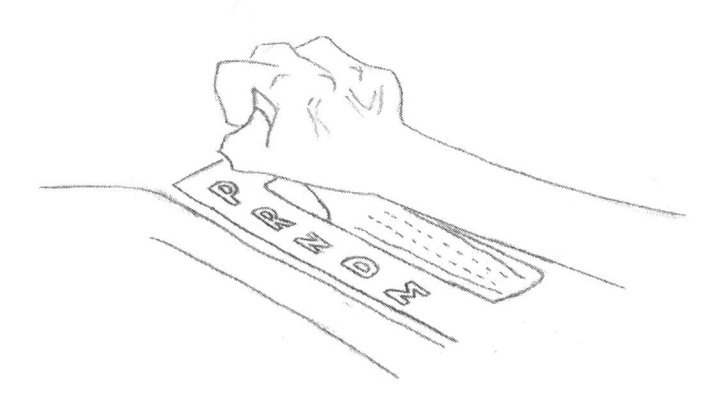

To Reality

Shifting

Prophecy

To

Reality

Written by

Patricia Stocker

2025

Dedicated to

The one who will never leave me nor forsake me my Lord and Savior, Jesus Christ. To those who are broken and tired of being tired. Let this book encourage you to go forward in life and not backwards.

Table of Contents

Introduction......................5

Anger............................9

Lost.............................31

Stolen..........................39

Different Angels of

..............Unhappiness.... ...35

Direction 63

Allow your Imagination to Run

Wild............................70

My Desire......................82

Prayer 83

Objective.......................84

Keep Silent……………....102

Accountability…..………....142

Informed……………...……120

Closing ……………..….…186

Reference……………………144

Introduction

Hello, to those who have decided to read this short yet powerful book. My name is Patricia, and I live in a small town in Florida where the idea for this book was born. Before we begin our journey in earnest, I would like to share some personal things to help familiarize myself to you!

Here are some quick notes about me:

- I am a mother of three
- I love being at the beach, and I especially love watching the waves as they fade away one after the other. Nothing helps to relax me more than watching the waves get

smaller and smaller one after the other. The water soon flows back out of sight and drift straight into my mind.

- I do have a college education that was not easy to come by. Education is encouraged in our family.

- My Sunday mornings and often Sunday evenings are spent in church.

This book is not meant to be long as it aims to reach all age groups. I realize in today's world attention spans are short, and it is best to get the point quickly!

However, the goal of this book is to help inspire and uplift, It is my hope and prayer the following words will serve as a bridge to your next phase in life. Enjoy!

Anger

I was tired of going to women conferences looking for hope yet returning home still hopeless. The time spent at these events was time that I could have used crossing off things on my to-do list: cutting grass, or doing laundry. I was tired of putting money into offering plates, and putting gas in my car, only to drive home with both less money and less inspiration than before.

I was tired of participating in group meetings and pouring out the most painful feelings in my life-feelings I had purposely buried, feelings I alone would have to deal with at night when those groups of strangers were no longer there to offer a comforting nod.

Groups are nice until you are alone with the thoughts you are forced to share there. Thoughts that keep you up at night, and rob you of precious sleep, sleep used to give your brain and heart a rest.

Opening old wounds, I thought were healed was like

having invasive surgery and cutting into the same spot years later—for no other reason other than entertaining a gallery of people who were already tired and ready to go away from the event. Now that spot too needs healing, even if the trauma was not as strong as the initial cut. It still hurts.

The idea that God *has more in store for me* can Sometimes drive me to my knees with helplessness. *What does he want me to do? Where does he want me to go? Why do I have these thoughts of doing better or overcoming unwanted circumstances in my mind? How am I going to get to my destination now that I have a desire to change?* These are all questions that I have asked myself time and time again.

How can I please God with the choices for my life, is a question that preachers have been trying to answer for many years. I believe that we as Christians forget that God wants us to be happy, *but include him in every aspect of our life.*

Figuring out what to do with my life and still encourage others to do the same is my goal with this book.

Far beneath the surface lies a place that is just between me and God, so sharing my feelings and thoughts with strangers who would not be there for me that night when I am re-living those memories alone, again and again. They would not be there for me when the tears begin to flood my face or the insecure feelings overwhelm me. All I was accomplishing was opening old wounds that were healed and now in need for a new healing because of re-injury. It was kind of like having surgery and many years later taking a knife and cutting into the same spot for no reason other than entertaining a group. That spot too now must be healed; recovery might not be as painful as it was the first time because the body remembers pain and adjust accordingly but it is still painful.

Christians forget that God wants us to be happy, but include him in everything that we do. God wants to be included in every aspect of your life. "In *all thy ways acknowledge him, and he shall direct thy paths" (Proverbs 3:6, KJV).* A simple motto to live by is this: if God cannot be there then neither should you. Long before the slaves were set free in the United States of America, God gave everyone the freedom of choice. We are free to choose what we want to do and who we want to be on this side of life.

There was once a man who had confessed that God had called him to preach the Gospel of Jesus Christ, and he never told a soul until he was dying. He spent all that time with a desire to preach, but did not have the tools or the time to go forward with his calling. He died with regret and great sadness. I do not know how he reconciled that with God as it was not my business. Thank you, God, for keeping me in my lane. I could not make the decision for him- it was his life to live and not mine.

The question of "Where does God want me to go" is a little more difficult? The Holy Spirit normally takes over and points us in the direction that God wants us to go.

"Howbeit when he, the Spirit of truth, is come, he will guide you into all truth" (John 16:13, KJV). It can be hard distinguishing the Holy Spirit

from our own wants and desires. Normally it is that still small voice that keeps urging you to go here or there. "It is one thing to speak to God. It is another thing to listen to God. When we listen to God, we receive guidance from the Holy Spirit" (Ortberg, p.140, 2002).

How many times have you had a thought to re-connect with someone only to make an excuse not to and live to regret it after something happens when the re-connection is no longer feasible? Other times we let profit get in the way of making sound choices. *what am I going to gain from this choice? Will I make more money or will I get a reward that is worth my sacrifice for making this choice?*

Leaving our comfort zone and branching out in new directions is a difficult decision, but most times it is well worth the discomfort we feel deciding to leave the comfortable place behind.

Any Prophet that is worth a grain of sand can tell you that they can only see part of the picture. No one knows it all, that honor belongs only to God.

"For we know in part, and we prophesy in part" (1 Corinthians 13:9, KJV).

Therefore, the prophecy that is proclaimed over your life is like a piece to a puzzle. The truth is if the true prophet sent by God sees it, it shall come to pass regardless if you accept it or not.

There was once a prophecy made to a man that was in his church, *("The prophecy was there would be people coming from all around to be in service with him).* The preacher took that to mean that he should accept a church that had called him to be their pastor. There was a terrible accident in his area and multiple people from one family were killed. There followed an enormous funeral attended by people from all over the world. The parking lot was overflowing with vehicles. Vehicles with state tags as diverse as the attendees themselves. Therefore, if the pastor was counting on the numbers in the prophecy to be recurring, he would have been disappointed. The Prophecy was true but those people would not be in attendance for service on a weekly basis. Therefore, if the pastor was counting on the numbers in the prophecy to be reoccurring, he would have been disappointed.

The anger or the frustrations that is dealt with in the church is from a, lack of knowledge. Not knowing how to accomplish a prophecy or a dream has become a real problem in the house of God. Yes, I know if the prophecy is from God, then he will fulfill it.

However, many times God sends people into our lives to help us with that very prophecy and we knowing "everything" will not accept their help/input.

We have a new level of hurt from the deaths that we have had to endure in the past few years or longer with unexpected deaths of loved ones who contracted the Covid 19 Virus.

Many people were not financially ready or spiritually ready to depart this life.

Anger causes one to lash out at others in hurtful ways and this causes more disruption in the church. I believe that there is a way that we can prosper in the House of God. I believe that we can turn that anger into a working tool and use it for our good.

Share the thing that you are angry about in your world.

_____

_____

_____

_____

_____

_____

35

Lost

I have so much that I want to do and say, but how do I do it? How do I get the chance to say it.? Those questions had been nagging me for years. Who do you trust with the desires of your heart? Who will value your inner thoughts like you do? The frustration of not knowing can drive a person to move too soon or too slow.

Life is funny in the way that it makes us search for answers that were within reach all the time.

What is it that keeps you going day after day year after year? What is it that drives you, or makes you say that "one day I am going to do this or that?" For me it was to go to college.

Every night before I went to bed I thought about college. Every day while working at my job, *I would say this is not what I want to do one day I am going to go to college.* At that time, I worked as a security guard. Being a security guard was never my dream, but it did pay my bills and put food on the table for my family.

I was lost from a lack of knowledge; I had no clue how to get from point **A** to point **B**. I was an adult and had no friends to call on for help, the assistance that you get in high school certainly did not help me prepare for making decisions about my life. I was now divorced with three children and dis-satisfied with my life. *Who* *could I go to for help, what book could I read that would help me?* I was just lost in space and time with no energy to even try moving forward. The fear was beginning to wear me down.

"Fear weakens us, causes us to be self-centered, and clouds our minds so that all we can think about is the thing that frightens

us. But fear can only control us if we let it" (Anderson, 2000, p. 216).

Being lost is not the worst thing that can happen to you, in fact it gives me hope knowing I, or you can be found.

"For the Son of man is come to save that which was lost" (Matthew 18:11, KJV).

Covid 19 has left many people with the feelings of helplessness and a loss of perspective.

Have you ever felt lost in your own life? Tell me about it.

_____

_____

_____

_____

_____

Stolen

I wanted to go to college but to do so I needed to find out how to get to college with no money. I did not seem to have any direction or clarification on anything. I felt as if my ex-husband had stolen not just my youth but also my joy.

"By ignoring scores of hurting people because their injuries

remain invisible to us, we are creating a new generation of hurtful people. When pain is real, the wounds are also real, even though they remain unseen" (Wilson, p. 26, 2001).

Perhaps you are one whose life was stolen by someone you trusted and loved. Perhaps a lifetime of servitude has been taken by a husband, a brother, a parent, a sister, or a wife. They got what they wanted from you, and you are left feeling used all up and now they are ready to get rid of you. The once youthful body and mind are gone along with that person's affections that you had, is all gone. The bright ideas that you once had to better your family has been used by someone else -- there is no more use for you.

What about the parent that uses the adult child but never really loved them, as their heart lies with your other siblings? It was you who they used to run their errands and take care of them when they got sick, and now it is also you who must look around to find that they have stolen your youth again. It is a sad realization learning you cannot go back and reclaim your youth. You cannot go back and have the tubes that were tied and burned re-attached so that you can give another man the son of his dreams.

"In spite of the unpleasantness, disappointments and daily trials I experience, I can carry on.

The demands that I be joyful and energetic at all times are unrealistic, and Jesus died on the cross so I can be unashamed to be real. I'm not a failure because I feel bad at times. I am a born-again child of God with a Savior who saves me from my own demands and expectations of myself and others" (Backus, Chapman, 2000, p. 181).

Have you ever felt that part of you has been stolen? Tell me about it.

_____

_____

_____

_____

_____

Different Angles of Unhappiness

Marital Woes

Part of being unhappy is not knowing what makes us happy. Perhaps you are in an abusive relationship and you have finally had enough. Your partner who takes their frustrations out on you, never has a kind word to say. You wake up in hell every morning

and go to sleep in hell every

night. The pillow that you rest

your head on every night is wet

from the tears that fall from

your eyes. You now have

children and nowhere to go; you

cannot tell anyone how

miserable you really are

because they would not

understand that even though he

treats you like the gum that is stuck to his shoe you still love him/her.

"The heart is deceitful above all things, and desperately wicked: who can know it" (Jeremiah 17:9, KJV)?

Your life is so depressing that you are embarrassed to tell anyone how things are in your home. The sad eyes that were once new have become permanent. The gleam that was once there is gone. The friends that you once had in high school are long gone. How do you heal from mental and/or physical abuse? *"Healing is not complete until that healing restores our wholeness" (Hart, p.253, 1999).*

Do you have marital woes or know someone who does? What message would you like to tell them, share?

_____

_____

_____

_____

_____

_____

Writer

    There was a time when you made good grades in English and you think that maybe you want to become a writer. You can rephrase any sentence and make it better; the gift of writing seems to be in your blood. Writing comes easy for you and the idea has been lying dormant in your soul for some time. Every time you see a movie, you think of more effective ways certain scenes could be done. *If that newspaper article had been written differently more people would have been interested in the article.* The notes that you leave for other people are poetic and should be kept and treasured by those who read them.

"Write the vision, and make it plain upon tables, that he may run that readeth it" (Habakkuk 2:2, KJV).

Is there a book or an article in you that needs to come out? Share it with me.

_____

_____

Preacher

Following in your grandfather's footsteps as a preacher is all that you have ever wanted from the time you were a little boy until now. You are now fifty years old and the thought still lingers in your heart to become a preacher one day just like your grandfather. He never made much money at preaching, so you decided to go into a different field to pay your bills. The children are all grown up now, and you have retired from the post office- your life is pretty good. Though you can live comfortably on retirement, something nags at you from time to time. It is hard to shake the idea of being a preacher like your grandfather once was. You cannot seem to even tell your wife how a childhood dream has resurfaced with a renewed intensity.

"And he said unto them, Go ye into all the world, and preach the gospel to every creature" (Mark 16:15, KJV).

Did it ever cross your mind to preach the Gospel of Jesus Christ? Make a choice now and write it here first.

_____

_____

_____

_____

_____

_____

The dreams of doing something different lie in the heart, but the know-how has felt far from reach until now. Now there is a clear path to our dreams and goals.

Above there were three different examples of life that many can relate to. Perhaps not in the specific examples, but within the feelings. This workbook shows any individual how to get started in a new direction.

Are you faced with a desire to make a change in your life? Tell me about it.

_____

_____

_____

_____

_____

77

Direction

What do all these things have in common, why are they grouped together? The one common thing that they all have is a lack of a plan or goal for themselves. They all are stuck in a situation that they would like to someday change sooner than later. While they are thinking about someday, life is passing them by- the clock never stops ticking. Soon everyone will leave the time and age that they are in and move on to another phase in life.

"To everything there is a season, and a time to every

purpose under the heaven"

(Ecclesiastes 3:1, KJV).

I am proposing that we can choose to be happy and be fulfilled in the phase of life we are in right now.

We have just made our first step: daring to dream about a different life. The dream may mean nothing to others even those that are close to you; but it is a lifeline to you right now. Others may not feel the desperation that you are feeling. They may have no idea that you are unhappy, because you have been able to disguise it for years. The odd thing is that you have been supporting others all your life in their ideas or dreams, but no one took the time to even ask you, what do

YOU have a passion for. Every time you get on the verge of telling them what you want to do with your life, they change the subject. We are now going to focus on our lives and how to be fulfilled in them!

Allow your Imagination to Run Wild

Write down all the things that you want to do in life. No matter how big or small they might be write those things down.

Write down all the places you wanted to go in life. When you were younger what did you say you wanted to be when you grew up?

The spaces below are for you to write down all your possibilities. Go ahead and allow your imagination to run wild.

_____

_____

_____

_____

Imagine New Life

Write it Down

1._____

_____

_____

_____

2._____

_____

_____

_____

3._____

_____

_____

_____

4._____

_____

_____

_____

5._____

_____

6.

7.

8. _____

_____

_____

_____

9. _____

_____

_____

_____

_____

10. _____

_____

11.

12.

13.

14.

15._____

_____

_____

_____

16._____

_____

_____

_____

17._____

_____

_____

18._____

_____

19._____

_____

20._____

_____

Now, let us take those imaginations and narrow them down to 10 possible ideas that you have given serious thought to. Let us write them down!

Possibilities

1. _____

   _____

   _____

   _____

2. _____

   _____

   _____

   _____

   _____

3. _____

_____

_____

_____

4. _____

_____

_____

_____

5. _____

_____

6. _____

7. _____

8.

9.

10.

Ten still seem to be a lot to focus on pick out five of the ten things above and write them down. We will call them Possible

---

Possible

1._____

2._____

3._____
_____

4._____
_____

5._____
_____

Now out of the five you have chosen above pick out three that you would like to pursue if you had the time and the money. Now write them down.

Probable

1._____

_____

2._____

_____

3._____

_____

Now out of the three you have chosen pick the most special item. The single choice you would chase if you knew this life was going to be over in a year and this is your last opportunity to accomplish anything of value in this life. THIS is what you

want to do. Write it down.

My Desire

1._____

_____

Prayer

Dear God Bless my Desire to come to light. Open my mind and my heart that I may receive instructions from you on how to go forward and complete this task that you have set before me. As I hear from you, give me the courage to do as you say. Please let my desire become a Reality as I move forward with all that I have written. In Jesus name I pray.

AMEN

Desire becomes Objective

Now in detail write down your objective. Make it as clear as possible to yourself. Write everything about the goal you want to accomplish. Take in account the time line, your finances, the location, your physical health—your age, anything necessary to make the objective a reality.

My Objective/Goal

_____

_____

_____

_____

_____

_____

_____

_____

_____

Groups are important to all objectives, even when it is an individual endeavor. We need people to help us when we are trying to accomplish things that are dear to our hearts. A <u>group</u> of people that put the President of the United States in office. A <u>group</u> of people that come together to give our children an education (teachers). It is a group of people who assemble themselves together in church to make the church what it is. It is a group of churches that come together to make an Association and a group of Associations that come together to make a convention.

Groups become very important as you continue your education. The grade you get is from the work that is put into the group activity. Whatever grade one person get the whole group gets.

Choose three partners to help you with your objective. There will be a total of four people in your group. Put their names and phone numbers on the first four spaces. These three people you choose do not have to be your friends or people you are close to. Think of it this way: Jesus had an inner circle that included three of his disciples (Peter, James and John), but 12 disciples in all. Therefore, a group of 12 or more may participate.

"And after six days Jesus taketh Peter, James, and John his brother, and bringeth them

up int a high mountain apart" (Matthew 17:1, KJV). The group of four will get together more frequently than the larger group of 12. The group of four will talk weekly encouraging one another helping to make decisions regarding your objective.

The larger group will get together monthly to compare

notes to make sure that everyone is on track with their objectives. Remembering to always encourage one another to push forward for their objective is just ahead of them waiting to be reached!

Partner/s

Name:

_____

_____

_____

Phone:

_____

_____

_____

Name:

_____

Phone:

Name:

Phone:

Name:

Phone:

The next set of lines is for the rest of your group if larger than four.

Name:

_____

_____

_____

Phone:

_____

_____

_____

Name:

_____

_____

_____

Phone:

_____

_____

_____

Name:

_____

Phone:

Name:

Phone:

_____

_____

_____

Name:

_____

_____

_____

Phone:

_____

Name:

Phone:

Name:

_____

_____

_____

Phone:

_____

_____

_____

Name:

_____

Phone:

Name:

Phone:

Name:

Keep Silent

Now is not the time to share your objective with every one, **keep silent**. People will discourage you, steal your ideas and make them their own or work against you to keep you from prospering. The time will come when you can share with others what you have accomplished, but now please do not discuss your goal with anyone outside of your group.

Group members do not share someone else's objective with others. That objective is the story that they are entitled to share, not you. Confidentiality is a lesson that we all learn as we grow in life. Everything is not meant to be shared right away.

Opening your mouth to the wrong person at the wrong time could cause harm that can never be repaired. Please, please keep silent about what is going on with your group. A day of celebration will come soon enough. A year is a good time to set for coming back and discuss the success and the failures. Then, you celebrate and move forward.

If you are thinking that you have too many people to put into groups that is where you are wrong. Any large number can be broken down to smaller numbers.

"And we will take ten men of a hundred throughout all the tribes of Israel, and a hundred

of a thousand, and a thousand out of ten thousand" (Judges 19:10, KJV).

It is much easier to talk to leaders of the groups, especially when there is one objective for everyone. Such as a project for a community or a project for a church.

Accountability

The reason you have partnered with someone is for accountability. Your partner(s) will help you to stay focused and to help move you forward -- especially during the days when you want to give up and walk away from it all.

"And he called him, and said unto him, How is it that I hear this of thee? Give an account of thou stewardship: for thou mayest be no longer steward" (Luke 16:2, KJV).

However, do not worry we all have to give an account to someone, this is nothing new. If you are a working individual then you may have to talk to your boss about your job. If you are married you communicate with your spouse about things that concern said marriage.

The same thing goes for parents. The state holds you accountable for your children. They must be clean and fed. They must live in a decent home.

Most importantly we all must give an account for our stewardship to God. We are more apt to finish our goals when other people are involved.

Being sick is not a reason to quit. Press on no matter how hard it might be or how tired you are.

"Bretheren, I count not myself to have apprehended: but this one thing I do, forgetting those things which are behind and reaching forth unto

those things which are before. 14: I press toward the mark of the prize of the high calling of God in Christ Jesus" (Philippians 3:13-14, KJV).

Remember this objective is for you and you alone. Keep moving forward, no matter how stressed out you may be.

Keep moving forward. Group members do not settle for incomplete answers. If they are too sick to move forward then rally around them and see what can be done to help move them forward!

With the scare of Covid 19 zoom or conference

calls will work just as well for communicating with partners. Now zoom is a preferred way to communicate in many groups.

In the military people come together from different backgrounds. They learn to walk as one, talk as one, and sleep as one. They may not know each other's name or even know each other's background, but they have a job to do. No one gets to quit until the job is done.

Back to me going to college, I started going to the local college to pick up brochures about becoming a student. There it was laid out for me: the first steps I had to take to get started. I applied for a grant and got it. I quit my job and became a full-time student. Two years later I had my first degree in computer Science.

Mark 1:40-45

40: And there came a leper to him, beseeching him, and kneeling down to him, and saying unto him, If thou wilt, thou canst make me clean.

41: And Jesus, moved with compassion, put forth his hand, and touched him, I will; be thou clean.

42: And as soon as he had spoken, immediately the

leprosy departed from him, and he was cleansed.

43: And he straitly charged him, and forthwith sent him away;

44: And saith unto him, See thou say nothing to any man: but go thy way, show thyself to the priest, and offer for thy cleansing those things which

Moses commanded, for a testimony unto them.

45: But he went out, and began to publish it much, and to blaze abroad the matter, insomuch that Jesus could no more openly enter into the city, but was without in desert places: and they came to him every quarter (Mark 1:40-45, KJV).

Those things which Moses commanded are found in Leviticus 14:1-32 (KJV)

4. Then shall the priest command to take for him that is to be cleansed two birds alive and clean, and cedar wood, and scarlet, and hyssop.

5. And the priest shall command that one of the birds

be killed in an earthen vessel over running water.

6. As for the living bird, he shall take it, and the cedar wood, and the scarlet, and the living bird in the blood of the bird that was killed over the running water.

This goes on until verse 32 the steps of being declared clean. Being declared clean meant that one could go and be amongst family and friends and no longer declared an outcast. That he could work for his living and not have to beg for scraps. Taking the steps to get home was worth every step that he had to make to be declared clean or healthy again.

Informed

Research

Do some research and find out about your objective. Count the steps necessary to make this objective a reality. Go to the library if you must. Scour the internet to find answers about your objective. Find at least five steps that your partner must take to make their goal a reality.

EXAMPLE:

Objective: To lose weight

1. Talk to my doctor to see if I need to lose weight

2. Find out how much weight do I need to lose

3. Finding a diet, I can stick to

4. Changing my diet, my food intake

5. Making an exercise program that suits my needs

   a. Walking 1 mile a day

   b. 20 Jumping jacks

   c. 10 push ups

   d. 50 stomach crunches

Some goals will have a great deal more than five steps. Another partner may bring five different ideas to the group.

Steps for partner: Buying a car

1. Check finances and see how much money willing to pay for car.
2. Apply for a loan if need be

3. Decide what make and model of car they would like

4. Decide what color of car they want

5. Decide if they want a new or used car

Find five steps that will help your partners get started with their objectives. Volunteer for objectives that you want and see if that is still something that you want to pursue, if not then there is still time in the first month to choose from your list of three. Choose something and see it through to the end of the year.

The greatest prophecy written by Jesus Christ is, *"Verily, verily I say unto you, He that believeth on me, the works that I do shall he do also; and greater works than these shall he do; cause I go unto my Father" (John:14 12, KJV).*

Now that you have the tools you can do greater things in the name of Jesus.

The steps that it will take for my Objective

Step 1

_____

Step 2

Step 3

Step 4

_____

Step 5

_____

_____

Step 6

_____

Step7_____

_____

Step 8

_____

Step 9

_____

Step 10

_____

Step 11

_____

Step 12

_____

Step 13

_____

Step 14

_____

Step 15

_____

Step 16

_____

_____

_____

Step 17

_____

Step 18

Step 19

Step

20 _____

_____

_____

Step

21 _____

_____

_____

Step

22 _____

_____

Step

23 _____

_____

_____

Step

24 _____

_____

_____

Step

25 _____

Step

26

My Partners five steps

Partner (1)

Name_____

_____

_____

1._____

_____

_____

2._____

_____

_____

3._____

_____

_____

4._____

_____

_____

5._____

_____

_____

Partner (2)

Name_____

_____

_____

1._____

_____

_____

2._____

_____

_____

3._____

_____

_____

4._____

_____

_____

5._____

_____

_____

Partner (3)

Name

_____

_____

_____

Partner (4)

Name

1._____

_____

_____

2._____

_____

_____

3. _____

_____

_____

4. _____

_____

_____

5. _____

_____

_____

Set Backs

Extra Thoughts

181

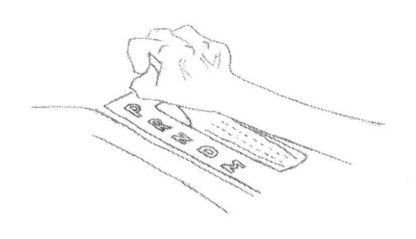

Closing

Are you one who can feel their dream slipping away? Can you feel the sun going down in your life? Has your life been stuck in reverse for so long that you feel going backward is normal?

You maybe have thought that being neutral is the right way to go. Maybe not taking a stand has been working for you, but

are you happy being less than

what God desires for you.

Maybe you have been at park so

long that you forgot that you

have a voice.

I have **Parked** my life and put it on hold. I have **Reversed** my way of thinking to accommodate others. I have been **Neutral** when I felt that both sides were wrong and my voice did not matter. However, today I am in **Drive** and will not be stopped by my fears. I am moving in the direction that God is leading me and oh what joy I feel from his presence.

Come and join me.

    Growth and brokenness are common in the church setting. The sad thing is if you do not have a personal relationship with Jesus the Christ then you may mis understand many things in the Christian arena. Growth in your heart and mind is what is being measured. Not the amount of people who may or may not grace the Sanctuary on Sunday morning. "Not that I speak in respect of want: for I have learned, in whatsoever state I am, therewith to be content" (Philippians 4:11). Commitment to the church in many ways is like being committed to your spouse. If one has never been faithful to their spouse then they have not learned the most valuable lesson about God or life. I take great pride in knowing that I never cheated on my Husband when I was married. Sure, temptations were there but my wedding vows meant something to me. The vows were not just mere words being said at a special occasion.

When you can still love the person who talked negatively about you to someone else or has called you everything but a child of God. That is called love, commitment and growth.

This project is not designed for you to finish in one day, or one week and some may not even finish in one year. However, you will be well on your way to accomplishing your objectives. The sleepless nights will be worth the prize at the finish line. The tears shed are worth the prize at the finish line. You have shifted your direction onto a path of fulfillment. You now have the skills to accomplish anything in your life. You know that if God did it before then he will certainly do it again.

"From now on wherever you go, or wherever I go, all the ground between us will be Holy Ground" (Nouwen, p. 45, 1986).

The works that you will have done over the period of a year will shift this prophecy into reality. It only takes a small move to shift or change a situation. The shift turns out to be just what some are looking for. Just think about a person who has trouble walking and they walk with a limp sometimes for them to walk straight only takes a small shift in their posture to change their status of handicap to a healthy individual.

May God bless each of you and strengthen you on your journey. May his loving arms of mercy surround you and may his grace keep you until we meet again. I pray that all of you take this workbook very seriously and in turn are enjoying Shifting Prophecy to Reality.

Take your first step

Blessing

Reference:

Anderson, N. (2000). The Bondage Breaker. Eugene, Oregon. Harvest House Publishers.

Backus, W. & Chapian, M. (2000). Telling Yourself the Truth. Minneapolis, Minnesota Bethany House Publishers.

Hart, A. (1999). The Anxiety Cure. Nashville Tennessee. Thomas Nelson Inc.

Nouwen, H. (1986). Reaching Out, the Three Movements

Of the Spiritual Life. Bantam Doubleday Dell Publishing Group.

Ortberg, J. (2002). Life You've Always Wanted. Grand Rapids, MI. Zondervan.

Wilson, S. (2001). Hurt People Hurt People. Discovery Grand Rapids, MI. House Publisher.

Special Thanks To

Melissa Hill M. ED., for your encouragement and for your help with my research. Thank you

Robert E. Gray M. MKT., for supporting me I never would have self-published if you had not said I could do it. Thank you

Robert S. Gray D. M., for always being there for me no matter how rough the road was. Thank you

Freddie L. Gray., for just being available to talk

My team of dreamers

Willie J. Blue D. M.

Courtney Stocker

R. Alex Gray Editor

Alan Cooper

He was the first person to encourage me to go forward with this book. Thank you Alan and I will never leave Ida out who has stood by me through all my years no matter what life has thrown my way.

Without you guys none of this would have happened. From the bottom of my heart to all of you. **Thank You.**

Thoughts

Made in the USA
Columbia, SC
20 February 2025